The Voice That
Changed the World

Culture Conflict

By

Eric F. Gilbert

ISBN:

978-1-968365-07-3

Index

Introduction

The name Charlie Kirk stirs strong emotions. To some, he was a polarizing voice who challenged cultural norms too directly. To others, he was a bold defender of faith, freedom, and the American experiment. But whether admired or opposed, he was impossible to ignore. This book is not written to add to the noise of soundbites or viral clips. It is written to ask a deeper question: Who was Charlie Kirk — really?

I have no intention of trying to sway your opinion of Charlie Kirk one way or another, just to clear the air and give a clear representation of who he was.

In the following pages, we will look at his life — from his childhood in Illinois to his rise as one of the most visible young conservative activists in the country. We will examine his values, the debates that defined him, and the controversies that shaped how he was seen. We will not shy away from the places where his words were cut, edited, or misunderstood. Nor will we ignore the lives that were changed because of them.

Charlie Kirk's story is not just about one man. It is about what happens when a generation begins to question, to push back, and to reclaim its voice. His life and message call us to wrestle with what freedom means, what faith requires, and what courage costs.

By the end, you may not agree with every stance he took. But you will see the man behind the headlines — and understand why his words continue to echo long after he is gone.

Foreword

There are moments in a person's life that reveal who they are more than any headline or sound bite ever could. For Charlie Kirk, one such moment came in a debate where he drew a simple but powerful comparison.

His point was that each year, nearly 50,000 Americans lose their lives in automobile accidents. It is a tragedy, but no one calls for banning cars. We accept that risk as the cost of a free society where people can move, travel, and build their lives.

Charlie applied that same reasoning to the Second Amendment. He reminded his audience that the right to bear arms was never about hunting or recreation. It was written into our Constitution to protect free citizens from the possibility of government tyranny. And just as we accept the risk of auto deaths for the freedom of mobility, we must accept the risk that comes with preserving liberty itself.

His critics clipped that moment, stripped it of context, and tried to turn it into proof of callousness. Yet anyone who heard the full exchange — anyone who knew Charlie — understood the truth. He wasn't glorifying tragedy. He was acknowledging reality: freedom is never free. It carries costs. And preserving liberty is worth those costs.

As you read it now, you can draw whatever conclusions you like, but at least you have the full story in front of you.

Another defining moment came when Charlie was asked whether he hated the LGBT community. The question was meant to corner him, to paint him as a bigot. Instead, his response reflected both his faith and his heart:

"I do not have hate for a group. I do not have hate for a people. How could I hate that which I have a heart for?"

He went on to point out that he did not agree with the lifestyle because of his faith, but he was very clear that his difference in beliefs did not change how he felt about a person.

That one line cut through the noise. It showed who Charlie really was. He stood firmly in his Christian convictions, often disagreeing with cultural trends and lifestyles. Yet he made it clear that disagreement is not hate. His guiding principle was love — love for his country, love for his faith, and yes, love for people, even those who disagreed with him the most.

These two debates — one about guns and liberty, the other about love and faith — tell the real story of Charlie Kirk. They reveal the strength of his convictions and the compassion of his heart. And they remind us why his words could be twisted by opponents, yet still inspire a generation to stand boldly for what they believe.

This book is not about the clips or the caricatures. It is about the man. It is about the ideas he stood for, the values he defended, and the movement he helped spark. It is about how his message continues to live on in the lives of those who now carry the torch.

Charlie Kirk's voice may have been silenced, but his legacy has only begun to speak.

Chapter 1:

Who Was Charlie Kirk?

Charlie Kirk was born on October 14, 1993, in Arlington Heights, Illinois, and raised in the suburbs of Chicago. From an early age, he showed a curiosity about the world and a drive to question what others simply accepted. That habit of questioning would later define his life. At Wheeling High School, he volunteered for a local congressional campaign. It wasn't glamorous work — knocking on doors, handing out flyers — but it gave him a taste of civic life. Politics, he realized, wasn't just something that happened in Washington. It was something ordinary citizens could influence.

When he was 17, Charlie wrote an essay for Breitbart News criticizing liberal bias in textbooks. It gained national attention and earned him an invitation to speak at the 2012 Republican National Convention. That moment thrust him into the national spotlight and convinced him that his voice could make a difference. Charlie briefly considered attending Baylor University in Texas, but he chose not to enroll. He believed his time was better spent in activism than in classrooms that he already saw as hostile to conservative thought. Instead, at 18 years old, he launched what would become his life's work.

The Birth of Turning Point
In 2012, Charlie founded Turning Point USA (TPUSA). What began as a scrappy startup with little more than determination soon grew into one of the most influential youth-focused conservative organizations in the nation.

TPUSA built chapters across high school and college campuses, trained young activists, and produced media content designed to engage a new generation. Under Charlie's leadership, it hosted major events like the Student Action Summit and the Young Women's Leadership Summit, drawing thousands of students and featuring some of the most prominent voices in conservative politics.

He expanded the mission with Turning Point Action, Turning Point Faith, and Turning Point Academy. These initiatives moved beyond the campus to influence churches, civic life, and even education. Charlie wasn't just building an organization — he was cultivating a movement.

Voice in Media and Writing Charlie reached millions through The Charlie Kirk Show, a daily podcast and radio program launched in 2019. His commentary mixed political insight with cultural critique and often climbed to the top of podcast charts.

He also authored three books:

Time for a Turning Point (2016), which laid out his vision for grassroots activism.

The MAGA Doctrine (2020), a defense of Donald Trump's movement.

The College Scam (2022), a sharp critique of higher education in America.

These platforms solidified him as one of the most visible conservative voices of his generation.

Faith   and   Family
While politics defined his public identity, Charlie's private life was shaped by faith and family. He married Erika Frantzve, a former Miss Arizona, entrepreneur, and outspoken Christian. Together, they had a daughter named Liberty — a living reflection of the values he often spoke about

on stage.
Charlie frequently spoke of fatherhood as his greatest responsibility. For him, faith and family were not add-ons to his activism; they were the foundation of it. He often said that the health of a nation began in the home, with strong marriages and present fathers. His own family life became both testimony and anchor for his work. Spiritually, Charlie was deeply connected to evangelical and non-denominational churches. He forged close bonds with pastors, especially Rob McCoy of Godspeak Calvary Chapel in California. Through Turning Point Faith, he encouraged churches nationwide to resist silence and take a bold role in civic life. His Christianity was not a private matter — it was the lens through

which he viewed politics, culture, and personal purpose.

Friends, Allies, and Critics

Charlie's influence gave him access to the highest levels of American politics. He aligned closely with Donald Trump Jr., Candace Owens, and a roster of Republican lawmakers. He served on Trump's 2020 advisory board and played a role in student voter outreach during the campaign. But his truest allies were often the students who lined up after events. Many nights, long after the cameras were off, he would stay behind to answer questions, listen to frustrations, or even pray with young men and women seeking direction. Of course, Charlie was also polarizing. His campus debates often drew both enthusiastic supporters and fierce protestors. To some, he was a bold truth-teller; to others, a provocateur. But even his critics could not ignore him. He became a figure impossible to overlook, whether admired or despised.

A Man Larger Than the Headlines By the mid-2020s, Charlie Kirk had become one of the most recognized conservative activists in America. Through Turning Point, his media platforms, and his public presence, he mobilized a generation of young people to speak with courage. Yet behind the stage lights, he was also a husband, a father, and a believer. Friends described him as disciplined, tireless, and willing to give himself fully to whatever task was in front of him — whether debating on stage, recording a podcast, or playing with his daughter.

He was a man of paradoxes: both warm and combative, both loved and hated, both mentor and lightning rod. What remained constant was conviction. Charlie Kirk lived his life as though truth mattered, courage was contagious, and freedom was worth defending.

Chapter 2:

The Values He Stood For

Charlie Kirk's public work was anchored in nine core values he repeated throughout his books, speeches, and debates. Each was not just an idea, but something he actively defended in front of audiences, critics, and students.

1. Faith in God

Kirk consistently tied his worldview to his Christian faith. In 2021 he said:

"I believe in the Bible, and I believe that Christ rose from the dead on the third day. This is the foundation of my faith and guides my actions."

(Charlie Kirk Show, Easter 2021 episode)

Faith was also institutionalized through

Turning Point Faith, launched to encourage churches to be more involved in civic life.

2. Free Speech

Kirk made free expression one of his central issues, especially on college campuses. In Time for a Turning Point (2016) he wrote: "Our generation must once again be allowed to speak freely, even if it offends someone. Free speech is the cornerstone of liberty." At TPUSA events, he frequently challenged what he called the "speech codes" of universities, encouraging students to debate openly.

3. Patriotism and the Constitution

Kirk repeatedly emphasized the Constitution as the safeguard of freedom. In a 2019 campus debate he said:
"The Second Amendment is not about deer

hunting. It is there, God forbid, so that you can defend yourself against a tyrannical government."

(University of Nevada, Reno, 2019)

He argued that patriotism meant both pride in country and defense of its founding principles.

4. Individual Responsibility

Kirk stressed self-reliance as a path to success. In his book The MAGA Doctrine (2020), he wrote:

"The American Dream is not given — it is earned. Hard work, discipline, and responsibility are the only true equalizers."

This theme was central in his debates with students who argued for more government programs.

5. Limited Government and Free Markets

From the beginning of TPUSA, Kirk's message was grounded in economic freedom. In Time for a Turning Point (2016), he wrote:

"Free markets, not government programs, are what lift people out of poverty."

At the 2018 Conservative Political Action Conference (CPAC), he told the crowd that "capitalism, not socialism, is the most moral economic system ever discovered."

6. Opposition to Identity Politics

Kirk often pushed back against group-based politics. At a 2019 University of Houston debate he said:

"I don't see people as members of groups. I see them as individuals created in the image of God. Identity politics tears us apart instead of bringing us together."

This was one of the most consistent themes in his college debates.

7. Pro-Life Advocacy

Kirk described abortion as a moral line that could not be crossed. At the 2022 March for Life rally, he said:

"There is no such thing as a moral abortion. Every abortion is wrong. Life begins at conception, and it must be protected."

This was one of his most uncompromising positions and a recurring focus of his speeches.

8. Skepticism of Higher Education

In his book The College Scam (2022), he argued that higher education was both overpriced and ideologically biased: "Universities are no longer places of learning — they are factories of conformity, debt, and indoctrination."

He urged young people to consider trade schools, entrepreneurship, or direct career paths instead of four-year degrees.

9. Defense of Traditional Values

Kirk often spoke about the importance of family and moral order. In The MAGA Doctrine (2020), he wrote:

"The strength of a nation is directly tied to the strength of its families. When families fail, communities fail, and the nation follows."

He connected this view to his Christian beliefs and his opposition to cultural shifts that he believed weakened family structures.

Summary

These nine values defined Charlie Kirk's public mission. Whether in a packed lecture hall, a national TV interview, or the pages of his books, he returned to these principles again and again. They explain not only what he believed, but why his supporters rallied to him — and why his critics often targeted him so fiercely.

Chapter 3:

The Power of Debate

Charlie Kirk built much of his reputation not in quiet writing, but in public debate. College campuses and packed auditoriums became his arena, where he fielded questions from critics, skeptics, and political opponents. His style combined quick recall of statistics, moral conviction, and a willingness to take on controversial issues head-on.

The Second Amendment
and Freedom's Cost

"Nearly 50,000 Americans die every year in automobile accidents. No one calls for banning cars. We accept that risk as the cost of mobility. The Second Amendment is far more important than the freedom to drive — it's there to protect citizens from tyranny. Liberty carries a cost, and we must be willing to accept that." (University of Nevada, Reno debate, 2019)

Race, Culture, and the Question of Fatherlessness

"You can be anything in America. The problem is not racism — it's culture. When fathers leave the home, everything falls apart. That's the number one problem in the Black community."

"You will never be the best version of yourself if you allow other people to convince you that you can't be better because of your skin color, because of your sexual identity, because of the community that you came from. If you truly want to be successful in America, you can be."

The George Floyd Debate

One of the most heated debates Charlie Kirk ever entered was over the death of George Floyd. During an audience Q&A, he was asked why he wanted the officer who "murdered George Floyd" pardoned. Kirk responded:

"George Floyd didn't die because of the police officer. He died largely because of a drug overdose… The knee on the neck is actually an approved police technique that police departments taught Derek Chauvin to use… His cause of death was not asphyxiation. It was drug overdose." Kirk went on to argue that the trial of Derek Chauvin was politically driven: "Our whole country blew up because of this incident and it was largely based on a lie. The lie is that there was a white police officer that went after a black person just cuz he was black, and it just wasn't true... This was largely a show trial... Chauvin was not even allowed to use the police training handbook in his trial to show that he was taught to use that restraining technique." Pressed on what he thought should happen, Kirk concluded: "Pardon. He should be free... It's a message that you should get an actual fair trial and that you're not going to get a trial by media."

Abortion: No Exceptions

"Abortion is murder. There is no such thing as a moral abortion." "We allow the massacre of a million and a half babies a year under the guise of women's reproductive health. That is how we got Auschwitz, that is how we got the greatest horror of the 20th century."

Faith and Love
in the Face of Accusation

"I do not have hate for a group. I do not have hate for a people. How could I hate that which I have a heart for?" (Turning Point USA Q&A, 2020)

Free Speech on Campus

"If your ideas can't survive open debate, then maybe your ideas aren't that strong. Free speech means I get to say things you might not like, and you get to respond. That's how it's supposed to work."

Economic Freedom vs. Socialism

"Capitalism is the most moral economic system ever discovered. It rewards service to others. Socialism, on the other hand, punishes success and enshrines envy as a virtue."

The Impact of Debate

For Supporters: He gave young conservatives a model of how to respond under pressure.

For Critics: He became a lightning rod, with his words frequently clipped, reframed, or spread without context — fueling the narrative that he was a divisive figure. But regardless of the audience, the debates amplified his influence and carried his ideas far beyond the lecture halls.

Chapter 4:

Taken Out of Context

Charlie Kirk's public career was marked by debates that went viral — but often not in the way he intended. Many of his most quoted lines were not shared in full, but cut down to fragments. The edits stripped away his reasoning and left only the most provocative sound bites. For critics, this fueled a narrative of extremism. For supporters, it revealed how determined opponents were to misrepresent him. I will show a few of the most common debates and how they were edited and you can draw your own conclusions.

The Gun Debate

Full Quote: "Nearly 50,000 Americans die every year in automobile accidents. No one calls for banning cars. We accept that risk as the cost of mobility. The Second Amendment is far more important than the freedom to drive — it's there to protect citizens from tyranny. Liberty carries a cost, and we must be willing to accept that."

Clipped Version: "We must accept gun deaths."

Purpose of the Edit?: By removing the car analogy and the constitutional context, critics reframed his argument as indifference to human life. In reality, his point was about the unavoidable tradeoffs of freedom.

On the Black Community

Full Quote: "You will never be the best version of yourself if you allow other people to convince you that you can't be better because of your skin color, because of your sexual identity, because of the community that you came from. If you truly want to be successful in America, you can be."

Clipped Version: "The problem in the Black community is culture."

Purpose of the Edit?: By cutting away the motivational appeal to individual potential, critics left only the harshest phrase. This allowed them to present him as dismissive of systemic racism, when his full point was about overcoming limiting beliefs and family breakdown.

The George Floyd Debate

Full Quote: "George Floyd didn't die because of the police officer. He died largely because of a drug overdose… The knee on the neck is actually an approved police technique that police departments taught Derek Chauvin to use… This was largely a show trial… Chauvin was not even allowed to use the police training handbook in his trial to show that he was taught to use that restraining technique… Pardon. He should be free."

Clipped Version: "George Floyd died of an overdose."

Purpose of the Edit?: By stripping away the references to training manuals, the broader argument about due process, and his call for a pardon based on what he called a "show trial," critics reframed his statement as pure denial of Floyd's suffering, maximizing outrage while minimizing context.

On Abortion

Full Quote: "We allow the massacre of a million and a half babies a year under the guise of women's reproductive health. That is how we got Auschwitz, that is how we got the greatest horror of the 20th century." **Clipped Version:** "Abortion is the same as the Holocaust." **Purpose of the Edit?:** The edit removed his reasoning and the numbers he cited, presenting him only as someone making a shocking comparison.

On LGBT Identity

Full Quote: "I do not have hate for a group. I do not have hate for a people. How could I hate that which I have a heart for?" **Clipped Version:** "I don't agree with their lifestyle."

Purpose of the Edit?: The cut eliminated the expression of love and humanity, leaving only the disagreement.

The Consequences of Misrepresentation Selective edits left many believing Charlie was a man of hate rather than conviction. Clips without context turned a Christian who spoke about love, responsibility, and freedom into a caricature of intolerance.

Yet a far different Charlie continued to shine through for those who watched beyond the clips. One man recently shared that his wife had bought him his first suit as an anniversary gift. Inspired by Charlie's words about manhood, faith, and family, he planned to wear it to church for the first time. He said Charlie's example stirred him to become a better man, husband, and father.

Charlie's legacy is not found in fragments, but in the full message he carried: faith, freedom, responsibility, and love.

Chapter 5:

Why They Feared Him

Charlie Kirk was not feared because he was violent, hateful, or merely loud. He was feared because he was effective. He had the courage to say what many whispered, the clarity to reduce complex arguments to plain truth, and the ability to give ordinary people permission to think for themselves. In a culture that rewards conformity and punishes dissent, that alone was revolutionary — and therefore dangerous to powerful interests.

He Spoke Where Others Stayed Silent He took questions others ducked and modeled responses under pressure, giving people a template for how to disagree respectfully, defend principle, and refuse intimidation.

Who "They" Are

The Cultural Managers; The Academic Gatekeepers; The Outrage Economy; The Bureaucratic & Institutional Complex; The Radical Fringe.

Each of these groups is weakened when individuals think for themselves, speak freely, and hold institutions accountable.

He Questioned the Approved Narratives

He challenged official storylines about race, policing, policy, and morality, refusing the premise that America is singularly defined by oppression or that speech must be curtailed for comfort.

He Spoke to the Next Generation

He spoke directly to young people, teaching them they didn't have to inherit the fatalism of prior generations.

He Exposed Hypocrisy

He named inconsistencies that many preferred to ignore.

They Feared His Defense of Free Speech

Free speech threatens managed narratives; a populace that argues back is catastrophic to those narrowing the range of acceptable thought.

They Feared the Return to Constitutional Fundamentals

People began rediscovering the rule of law, individual rights, separation of powers, free speech, property rights, and civic responsibility — the scaffolding that prevents unchecked power.

The Real Reason They Feared Him
They feared the courage he awakened in millions.

Consequences and Reckoning
Event cancellations, character attacks, media outrages, deplatforming campaigns — tactics meant to neutralize a movement demanding free inquiry and constitutional fidelity.

Closing:

What He Re-Ignited
He reminded a generation that the Constitution is a living guide for civic courage: speech matters, responsibility matters, liberty requires defense.

Chapter 6:

The Movement He Sparked

The shot that ended Charlie Kirk's life also set something in motion. What began as shock turned into action. What began as mourning turned into organizing. The movement isn't about what he did—it's about what countless people are doing because of him now.

A Surge in Local Mobilization

Not long after his death, cities and towns across America lit up with remembrance — vigils, memorials, even calls for statues.

In San Antonio, students and community members gathered under candles at UTSA's Sombrilla Plaza, turning grief into a public commitment to carry forward Kirk's message.

In Montgomery County, locals began fundraising for a statue to immortalize his influence in their community.

In Medina, Ohio, nearly a thousand people filled the public square to mourn, sharing stories, signs, and determination to act.

These events weren't one-off memorials. They became catalysts. Turning Point USA chapters reported surges in membership and interest. People who had followed from a distance started organizing locally. Faith communities picked up calls to pray and act. Local media outlets kept covering what was happening on the ground.

International Echoes

The energy did not stay within U.S. borders:

• **United Kingdom:**

Multiple vigils and rallies held in London.

At least one major rally in Whitehall drew between 110,000–150,000 people.

Turning Point UK leaders pledged to "pick up his torch" and continue his mission.

• **New Zealand:**

Māori Christians performed a haka tribute at a vigil.

Widely shared on social media as a symbol of respect and cultural honor.

• **South Korea:**

High-profile entertainers (e.g., K-pop idols, former Wonder Girls member Sunye) posted tributes to Charlie.

Some later deleted them after backlash, showing both the reach and the controversy of his influence.

Local Christian and conservative groups held prayer gatherings in Seoul, connecting his message to their own struggles for faith and free speech.

- **Japan:**

Just days before his death, Charlie toured Japan with nationalist party Sanseito.

After news of his death, Sanseito leaders and church groups in Tokyo and Osaka held memorial events, calling his passing "a loss for free nations everywhere."

- **Australia:**

Sydney and Adelaide both saw large park gatherings.

Sydney's Hyde Park vigil drew thousands, organized by Turning Point Australia.

Adelaide's Elder Park vigil combined hymns, prayer, and speeches — backed by local Christian media.

Organizational Growth & Momentum

Here's where it gets structural: this is about more than grief. It's about infrastructure.

After Erika Kirk's first public speech since the assassination, TPUSA received 18,000+ new chapter requests. That shows people aren't just mourning—they want to build.

Total new chapter requests across high school and college soared past 37,000.

Surge in volunteer and staff interest: many reaching out to help, to spread his message, to serve in Turning Point USA in varying capacities.

The Cultural Ripple Effects

Public symbols of remembrance are appearing: statues being proposed, rooms being dedicated (like a debate room in a London pub).

Music, social media, and art are all becoming vectors for his legacy: tribute songs, viral posts, and creative expression from local musicians.

People who had been dormant politically or spiritually are showing renewed interest: faith communities resurrecting civic engagement, families discussing values, students refusing to stay silent in school. The frontlines are local — in homes, campuses, civic clubs.

Why This Is Different

What distinguishes this movement is that its momentum came *after* his death. When someone passes, often people remember — but this has become more than memory.

It's institutional: requests for chapters, new volunteers, dedicated meeting rooms.

It's emotional and moral: sadness mixed with righteous anger and resolve.

It's global: communities overseas are mirroring what's happening in U.S. towns and cities.

It's ongoing: it hasn't slowed; if anything, the response is accelerating.

Closing: A Movement Alive

This movement isn't a relic of what Charlie Kirk once said. It lives in what people are *now* doing. The vigils and memorials are not ends but beginnings. Each new chapter request is a seed. Each artist's tribute song, each prayer service, each local group forming, every pub dedicating a debate room—these are echoes of his life, amplified.

The world he spoke into risked silence. But people chose voice. The uniforms of grief become badges of action. And the movement he sparked in sudden tragedy carries with it a promise: that conviction doesn't die with the person, but lives in the courage of thousands who rise.

Chapter 7:
A Call to Action

History does not wait for those who hesitate. The moment is always claimed by those who speak, act, and stand when others are silent. Charlie Kirk believed freedom's future would be decided by ordinary citizens who refuse to bow to fear. Regardless of which side you find yourself on in these debates, one thing that Charlie believed in that shines through it all, is the importance of free speech. So, take this time as a call to action speak up for what you believe in just like Charlie did. Not by hating those that believe differently from you, but by explaining the logic behind your beliefs, just like Charlie. That's the whole point of free speech!

Why Standing Up for Values
Matters Now

The daily struggles over education, truth, freedom, and responsibility demand engagement. Silence cedes to the field.

Practical Ways to
Step Into the Fight

Speak truth in your sphere; defend local free speech; strengthen your family; engage civically; build courage in others.

The Lasting Impact

His life is measured in the courage he ignited: students who speak, fathers who step up, churches that grow bolder, voices echoing faith, family, freedom, responsibility.

Closing Charge

What will you do now? If you speak and stand, his legacy lives on — and freedom remains the birthright of future generations.

Conclusion:

The Great Awakening

Across America, something is stirring. Ordinary people refuse to whisper what they believe. Families reclaim their role. Young people step forward, unafraid.

This is the fruit of truth planted through debate, sacrifice, and conviction. For every clipped video, there are uncut lives changed. For every slanderous headline, there are homes where fathers rise and students stand.

This movement is not about one man; it is about millions who choose to live without fear — a nation remembering its foundation and reclaiming its voice.

This is only the beginning. The Great Awakening is the sound of truth in hostile halls, the courage of new chapters, the prayers of families, and citizens rediscovering their Constitution.

History will not remember the critics who twisted his words, but the people who, inspired by him, chose to stand.

This is not the end. This is only the beginning.

References

Breitbart News. "Liberal Bias in Textbooks." Essay by Charlie Kirk, 2010.

Time for a Turning Point. Charlie Kirk. Humanix Books, 2016.

The MAGA Doctrine. Charlie Kirk. Broadside Books, 2020.

The College Scam. Charlie Kirk. Winning Team Publishing, 2022.

The Charlie Kirk Show (podcast and syndicated radio program). Various episodes, 2019–2025.

Turning Point USA official website and publications.

Public speeches and debates at U.S. college campuses, 2013–2025.

Interviews and media appearances, including Fox News, Newsmax, and other outlets.

Tributes & Movement After His Death

San Antonio Express-News. "Vigil at UTSA for Charlie Kirk draws hundreds." September 2025.

Houston Chronicle. "Montgomery County plans event to honor Charlie Kirk with statue." September 2025.

News 5 Cleveland. "Hundreds in Medina gather to mourn the death of conservative activist Charlie Kirk." September 2025.

Times of India. "Emotional farewell to Charlie Kirk at Washington memorial." September 2025.

Adelaide Now. "Prayer vigil at Elder Park for Charlie Kirk following Utah shooting." September 2025.

Daily Telegraph (Australia). "Crowd gathers to mourn Charlie Kirk in Sydney's Hyde Park." September 2025.

Facebook (Turning Point UK). "We will pick up his torch" — tribute to Charlie Kirk. September 2025.

YouTube. "Whitehall vigil for Charlie Kirk, London." September 2025.

Korea Times. "Tributes to Charlie Kirk spark controversy among Korean stars." September 2025.

India Times. "Fans call for Choi Siwon's exit after Charlie Kirk tribute." September 2025.

Reuters. "Days before death, Charlie Kirk debuted his conservative message in Asia." September 2025.

Facebook (Real Lexit). "New Zealand Māori Christians pay tribute to Charlie Kirk with haka at vigil." September 2025.

Fox News. "London pub dedicates room to Charlie Kirk after tragic death." September 2025.

Fox News. "Erika Kirk's first speech sparks surge in TPUSA chapter requests." September 2025.

Yahoo News. "Turning Point USA says campus chapter requests top 37,000 after Charlie Kirk's death." September 2025.

Fox Business. "Interest in working for TPUSA surges after Charlie Kirk's death." September 2025.

Author's Bio

Eric F. Gilbert is an entrepreneur, author, and speaker with more than 25 years of experience building businesses and mentoring leaders. He has founded and revitalized multiple companies across industries, from marketing and publishing to retail and manufacturing, and has taught thousands through books, webinars, and live events.

As the author of works including Broke to Business Boss, 5 Secrets Millionaires Don't Want You to Know, and They Lied About SEO, Gilbert has become known for blending practical strategy with motivational insight. His writing and speaking often focus on helping people cut through noise, see truth clearly, and take decisive action. Gilbert brings this same perspective to Who

Was Charlie Kirk?, approaching a controversial and influential figure with honesty, depth, and a commitment to clarity. He lives in Florida with his wife, Shana, where they continue to build businesses and inspire others.

www.ingramcontent.com/pod-product-compliance
Lightning Source LLC
Chambersburg PA
CBHW020759130626
46554CB00006B/2265